TRAFFIC BLAST!

The Incredible 31-Day Plan for Generating Massive Online TRAFFIC and Increasing Online Revenue!

Kit Elliott

ISBN: **978-0-578-06698-1**

Earnings Disclaimer: Do not invest in this or any book/training if you think it will automatically make you money just because you bought it. You have to work to succeed in anything (especially business) and I'm neither going to hide nor apologize for that. Results will vary. In the end, you may not make any money at all. It's possible you might even lose money. Know that before you going in, because if you're looking for the magic pie in the sky, I'm sorry but this ain't it.

http://www.KitElliott.com

http://www.SuperAffiliate.com

This book is dedicated to those

who believe in **freedom**…

A SHORT NOTE FROM THE AUTHOR

Hi there. I'm Kit Elliott.

I'm officially a "retired" 6th grade school teacher who makes a full-time income marketing products online. I believe that people should design their best life by setting up their businesses to blast "passive" income in their bank accounts no matter where they are or what time it is! After working 60 to 80 hours per week teaching 6th grade Science, I quickly realized that the full-time JOB income was not enough to cover my student loans and living expenses. When my nerve damage on the left side of my body kicked in, I had to make a quick decision that my health was more important than a long-houred, low-paying JOB. And that's when I spent my summers developing systems that sell products online, gain new customers, and **passive profits for life!**

Most of my products have a "continuity" plan built-in. That means that when customers sign up for hosting; I get a piece of the monthly hosting every month. That means that when businesses sign up for merchant accounts, I get a piece of the monthly fees every month. That means that when people sign up for "monthly" services that I recommended, then I get a piece of the residual every month for as long as they use the service.

The beauty behind this plan is simple: **Recommend services and products where people rarely cancel.** Think about it? When are people going to cancel their hosting? They can't unless they want their website to disappear. When are people going to cancel their merchant accounts? They can't unless they want their income to disappear..

And now, I help others quit their day jobs, and start living the life they WANT not the life they are forced to live because of "financial" reasons. I wrote this book for you. I purposely did not have it professionally edited because I wanted it to read like I'm having a personal conversation with you. As a former 6th grade Science teacher, **I use step-by-step examples and lots of ACRONYMS to help you remember and get value out of the book,** and at the same time, I don't want you to feel like you need a master's degree to understand the content of this book. I would rather you walk away with traffic than think of me as "THE MAN!" which, well, you can do both.

You can visit me at KitElliott.com, and let's talk about different online opportunities and strategies that help grow online businesses. I, now, have my own radio show published on iTunes and you can catch me every Monday for the Online Home Business Show! You can also signup for our affiliate program at SuperAffiliate.com!

I hope you truly enjoy the BLAST! series. When you are successful, please let me know so I can feature you on my RADIO show or even link back to your site.

Now, it's time!

It's time to create a BLAST of TRAFFIC to your site through my simple blueprint. Let's get this party started...

Onwards and Upwards,

Kit Elliott

Online Home Business Dude

If you would like to get a piece of the "residual" action, then join me for what I believe is the "NEXT BIG THING!" at www.ResidualRush.com ..

Your Daily TRAFFIC Blast! Blueprint

In The Beginning...

Hi, Kit Elliott here, and I'd like to welcome you to TRAFFIC BLAST! where you're going to discover my simple formula for getting TRAFFIC to your website and building your presence online!

As you already know –

The money IS in the list.

That's why some of the world's best marketers focus so much of their attention on growing their lists. And that's why I've created this TRAFFIC BLAST! Blueprint for you.

I'm very excited to follow you on your journey because over the next few dozen pages you'll discover some of the very best customer-building and online marketing *tricks*, *strategies* and *secrets*. And you'll also learn the **G.R.O.W.I.N.G.** formula for building a big responsive list of customers:

> G – **GIVE** prospects a reason to join your list.
>
> R – **REAP** the benefits of JV and affiliate marketing.
>
> O – **OPTIMIZE** your site for the search engines.
>
> W – **WRITE** articles.
>
> I – **INVITE** others to spread your marketing message.
>
> N – **NETWORK** on social marketing sites.
>
> G – **GET** started!

To make this formula even easier for you to follow, I've divided each part of the formula into multiple steps.

> **Quick Tip: You can complete one step each day – and since there are 31 steps in all, you'll be well on your way to building a huge, responsive list after just one month!**

Let's get started…

CHAPTER 1

The "G" in G.R.O.W.I.N.G.

GIVE Prospects a Reason to Join Your List!

Before you can actually start building your list, you need to prepare your lead-capture page (also known as "squeeze page") and autoresponder series.

As you'll discover in a moment, just posting a newsletter subscription form on your site isn't enough –

You need to actually give your prospects a REASON to join your list.

Conventional wisdom suggests that because your newsletter is free, people will come in droves to join your list... but that's simply NOT true.

Indeed, now more than ever –

People are actually somewhat afraid togive their email address to a stranger.

And that's because of the fear of having their address shared and spammed. As such, taking the time to write good sales copy will increase your conversion rate.

This part of the **G.R.O.W.I.N.G.** formula covers four days, where you'll learn:

- Day 1: How to create the squeeze page.
- Day 2: What sort of "bribe" you should offer prospects.
- Day 3: How to create an autoresponder series that builds a relationship with your subscribers.
- Day 4: How to avoid freebie seekers that are unwilling or unable to buy anything.

Day #1
Create a Compelling Squeeze Page

Your first step in building a big list is creating a lead-pulling squeeze page. To do that, you need the following elements:

1) A headline with a big benefit that also (preferably) arouses the reader's curiosity.

2) Body copy and a list of benefits that gives the reader a strong reason why they should join your list.

3) A strong call to action.

Let's look at each of these separately…

1) A Compelling Headline

Your headline is the most important part of your entire squeeze page. That's because if the headline doesn't do its job – which is to get the prospect to read the rest of your copy – then your entire squeeze page might as well not even exist.

Too often, marketers make the mistake of trying to sell their products, services and even free newsletter subscriptions in the headline. Don't even attempt it… you don't have enough room to do that anyway.

Instead, tempt your prospects with a compelling benefit and arouse curiosity in an effort to make them keep reading. Grab them by the shirt collar and drag them into their copy. If your headline "sucks" them into the rest of your copy, you'll have plenty of time to use your best persuasion tactics to get their subscription.

Example: "Discover FOR FREE How a 45-Year-Old Waitress Lost 30 Pounds Without Dieting… And How YOU Can Too!" This example includes a benefit and uses the word "free" (which is a trigger word, and arouses curiosity).

2) Reason-Why Copy and Benefit List

Once you've pulled your prospect into your copy, then you need to sell them on joining your list. That means giving them strong reasons why they should join, with a strong emphasis on a bulleted benefit list that catches the eye.

Think of your bulleted benefits like mini-headlines: Each of them should promise a benefit and, preferably, arouse curiosity.

Example: "Turn to page 12 to discover the common herb that wards off the common cold!"

In this section of your squeeze page you'll want to include proof of your claims as well as social proof such as testimonials from your other newsletter subscribers.

3) A Strong Call to Action

Finally, your squeeze page should end with a strong call to action. This is where you specifically tell your prospects exactly what you want them to do.

Common sense suggests that if you have a strong headline and strong, benefit-laden copy, then prospects would be eager to join your list – and they'd know exactly what to do. But tests have also repeatedly proven that telling prospects EXACTLY what to do increases your conversion rate.

Example: "Fill in your first name and email address below and click "submit" to join get your free weight loss report now!"

Day 2:
Create a Freebie to Encourage Prospects to Join Your List

The second thing you'll need to create is some sort of extra incentive for people to join your list.

Naturally, the newsletter itself should be a big draw (and thus you should fo-cus on the benefits of receiving the newsletter). However, ideally you should offer some sort of bonus – a freebie – to make signing up for your list a "no brainer."

What sort of freebie might you offer?

The answer rests with your target market:

What do THEY want?

- **What sort of problem do they have that you can solve?**
- **What sort of information are they desperate to get their hands on?**

> **Insider Tip:** *One of the best ways to create a more responsive list is by knowing as much as you can about your list members. If you know, specifically, what each of your subscribers prefer, then you can easily segment your list and send out highly targeted offers.*

You see, just because you're offering a freebie doesn't mean the value of the product should be low.

Quite the opposite.

Instead, you should be offering high quality content – something you could sell for at least $50. That way people will say, "look at what he's offering for free – just imagine what his paid products must be like!"

Here are a few suggestions for freebies you can deliver immediately when someone joins your list:

- **A free ebook or report.**
- **A free multi-day ecourse.**
- **Valuable software.**
- **An audio interview or other audio product.**
- **A valuable video.**
- **Tools like calculators or spreadsheets.**
- **Useful products like blog themes, screen savers, and similar.**
- **A free teleseminar (We use WealthWorldConnect.com)**
- **Free access to a "private membership site."**

- A free 10 or 15 minute consultation (be careful with offering services, unless you have a good paid upsell in place).

You may also consider requesting a physical mailing address alongside the email address. In order to easily get a physical address, your freebie may be something like a CD or DVD shipped in the mail.

One way to segment your list is to make a short checklist as part of the newsletter sign up. Simply ask your subscribers to check their interests from a list.

Example: Let's suppose you run a travel site. Your instructions might say, "What type of vacations interest you most? Please select all that apply from the following list:"

- Beach vacations
- Mountain vacations
- Ski vacations
- Luxury vacations
- European vacations
- US vacations
- Asian vacations
- Volunteer vacations
- Green vacations
- Cruise vacations
- …and so on.

Now you have the ability to write highly targeted emails. For example, if you're offering a discount vacation package on a choice of ski vacations or cruise vacations, you can use your segmented list to speak directly to your ski fans and your cruise fans.

You send one email to ski fans offering them a discounted ski vacation and you send another email to the cruise fans offering them a discounted cruise. Then you send a general offer to the rest of your list.

<u>End result?</u>

Higher conversion rates!

Test it for yourself and see how segmenting your list can boost your profits.

Day 3:
Create Your Autoresponder Series

If the freebie that goes along with your newsletter is a multi-part (multi-day) ecourse, then you already have this step covered. If not, then you'll need to create a series of at least 7-12 autoresponder messages for starters.

Autoresponder Service for Smart Marketers:
Smart Marketers are switching to WealthWorld Touch for all of their autoresponder needs. With reliable email deliverability and easy to use web forms, I use it for all my email autoresponder and broadcast service.
Visit WealthWorldTouch.com to take the $1 trial!

The reason for creating a series of messages is twofold:

1) **It helps you start building trust and a relationship (automatically) with your subscribers. People buy from those they know, like, and trust.**

2) **It also creates a stream of income for you, as you can start pitching products immediately in your autoresponder series. If you do not have an**

autoresponder service, then, online marketers are now switching to WealthWorldTouch.com.

As mentioned, you'll want to start with at least 7-12 messages. However, each week you should commit to adding a few more messages to your series.

That way you can have months of content – or even a year or more of content – all sent out AUTOMATICALLY to your subscribers.

Indeed, you can get to the point of having a nearly hands-free list (save for a live broadcasts that you send from time to time).

Because you are sending out content that may not be seen by your subscribers for months or even a year or more from now, your content needs to be "evergreen."

That means –

It needs to be just as relevant a year from now as it is right this month.

Example: Talking about the latest "fad diet" or about specific diet pills are NOT evergreen topics. However, talking in general terms about fad diets and diet pills – without mentioning any specific fads by name – would qualify as evergreen content.

Of course you can mention specific products (and link to them using your affiliate link) if they're time tested and likely to be around for a while. In other words, if the product themselves are evergreen.

Example: A good example of that is a copywriting book that goes over the basics of how to write a sales letter. While copywriters are always coming up with new ideas and spins on old ideas, the basics have stood the test of time and will be evergreen for as far into the future as you can see.

What Should You Include in Your Series?

The first thing you should include in your series is <u>whatever you promised subscribers on your squeeze page</u>.

That's your most important consideration initially – because if your subscribers don't get what they expect and what they were promised, they won't be subscribers for long.

Beyond that, your autoresponder series should be used to solve your market's most pressing problems.

1) Some of the problems you can solve for free via the content in your newsletter.

2) Other problems you can solve by recommending paid products.

In many cases you'll do both right in the same article.

Example #1: Let's suppose you have an article about how to correctly use diet pills to lose weight. The article itself is informational and in-demand by your market. But the article could also pitch a specific brand of diet pills, vitamins, or supplements through your affiliate link.

> *Example #2: Let's suppose you're writing an article on how to optimize a website for the search engines. The article could go through the basics of how to do it and yet it could include links to SEO (search engine optimization) tools like a paid subscription to WordTracker.*

Here's the take away point:

You don't have to "hard sell" in every email. Instead, weave recommendations and links for paid products into some of your free content.

> **A "Common Sense" Tip:** *NEVER recommend a product or service that you wouldn't recommend to your mother or your best friend.*
> *It doesn't matter how high the commission rate is, how amazing the conversion rate is, or how much money you can stuff in your pockets recommending it. If the product stinks, do **NOT** recommend it. Your reputation – and your future sales and income – depends on this.*

Day 4:
How to Avoid Freebie Seekers

So far you've learned how to set up your squeeze page to ensure the highest conversion rate possible. And in the coming pages you'll discover how to send hordes of eager subscribers to your newsletter.

All of that results in you having a BIG LIST.

But just as important as the size of your list is the RESPONSIVENESS of your list.

After all, a list of 100,000 people doesn't mean a thing if no one ever responds to your offers.

On the flip side, you can lead a decent live simply from the income coming from a small, highly responsive list. (Just imagine the kind of life you'll lead with a big, responsive list!)

The responsiveness of your list is dependent on a combination of several factors, including but not necessarily limited to:

- **How well you've attracted a niche market (rather than a general mass market group of subscribers). The more focused your niche, the better your response.**

Example: If you're running a dog training site, then you need to attract dog owners (whose dogs need training) to your site. Simply attracting "pet lovers" won't do. Nor will attracting dog lovers who don't have dogs that need training.

- **How targeted your mailings are. If you've attracted a niche market and you're sending out niche-oriented offers and emails, then you can expect a good response.**

- **How well you've built a relationship with your readers. People buy from those they know, like and trust.**

- **How well you write your offers (e.g., your copywriting skills). If you write good copy, you can expect a better response.**

There is one important (yet sometimes overlooked) subcategory that's related to focusing on your target market.

Namely –

**You need to be sure that you're attracting
<u>ACTUAL</u> buyers as opposed to freebie seekers.**

Think of it this way:

When you're targeting your market, part of your pre-qualification should be that your buyers are able, willing and even eager to buy products that solve their problems.

Otherwise you'll have a list of freebie seekers who drag down your conversion rate. And the true freebie seekers (those who want something for nothing) will even waste your time peppering you with questions (though they don't intend to buy) or they'll buy with the full intention of refunding instantly.

So how do you avoid freebie seekers?

Here are a few suggestions:

- **PULL in buyers, not tire-kickers.** If you're pulling in search engine TRAFFIC based on search terms with the word "free" in them, and if it seems like the whole focus of your site revolves around "free stuff," then your visitors will expect freebies. While it's OK to offer freebies for your prospects, just make sure the emphasis of your site is on the solutions you offer, rather than just the FREE solutions.

- **PUT the emphasis of your squeeze page on your newsletter and less so on the freebie.** If your emphasis is on the freebie itself, the freebie seekers may be tempted to give a "throw away" or temporary email address just to get the freebie.
  Instead, put the focus of your squeeze page on the benefits they'll receive from the newsletter. That way your subscribers will actually be eager to open and read each issue – and of course that increases your conversion rate.

- **PREPARE your prospects and set expectations.** Let potential subscribers know that your newsletter offers things like product reviews and comparisons, discounts coupons on products and similar. That gives potential subscribers a "heads up" that your newsletter isn't all about the freebies – and it gives buyers a huge incentive (benefit) to join your list!

- **PITCH paid products in the very first email you send out.** You don't have to hard sell in your emails. Instead, weave product recommendations into your content as described previously.

<u>Bottom line:</u> You don't have to "fear" freebie seekers as most of them are harmless. But neither should you go out of your way to attract them – especially if you're doing any postal mailings (which of course require a cash outlay in order to contact your prospects).

CHAPTER

2

The "R" in G.R.O.W.I.N.G.

REAP the Benefits of JV Marketing

Now it's time to discover how to start driving potential subscribers to your site. There are plenty of ways to do this, and you'll learn all about these over the rest of this ebook. For starters, however, you'll discover the secrets of using JV (joint venture) and affiliate marketing to drive hordes of prospects to your site.

DEFINED: "JV Partner" and "Affiliate Partner"

Although some people use the terms "JV partner" and "affiliate partner" interchangeably, there are differences.

An affiliate partner promotes your product for a commission.

A JV partner works with you on product creation, promotion, or other aspects of

> *Think about this for a moment: The point of your free newsletter is to build a list of likely buyers, right? So if someone comes to your site to view a paid product – even an inexpensive one – and they then join your newsletter, chances are they're interested in being buyers.*

your business for mutual benefit. It may be for a commission… or it could be for some other benefit such as publicity and exposure, backlinks, and similar.

While an affiliate can be a JV partner, not every JV partner is an affiliate.

The reason we're starting here is because there are no up front out-of-pocket costs (only commissions on sales) and the TRAFFIC tends to be highly targeted and VERY responsive.

Now you'll notice we're including "affiliate marketing" as part of this strategy, which of course involves affiliates recommending your paid product.

Maybe you're wondering how that works since you're offering a free newsletter, right?

As such, some of the most responsive newsletter subscribers you can get are those that come from affiliates or JV partners pitching your paid products.

Indeed, you may even want to give your partners 100% commissions just so you can enjoy building a big, responsive list from these likely buyers!

This second part of the *G.R.O.W.I.N.G.* formula covers five days, where you'll learn:

- Day 5: Where to find potential JV partners?
- Day 6: How to approach potential partners with an irresistible offer.
- Day 7: How to create an affiliate program that attracts super affiliates.
- Day 8: Where to find super affiliates?
- Day 9: How to approach affiliates.

Follow along on days five through nine as we go step by step through finding and approaching JV partners and affiliates…

Day 5:
Where to Find Potential JV Partners

There are a variety of places to seek out potential JV partners, which we'll list in just a moment. But no matter where you're looking, keep in mind what it is, exactly, what you're looking for in a JV partner.

Example #1: If you're looking for product creation help, then a JV partner with name recognition in the niche would serve you well. You can borrow that person's credibility through association.

Example #2: On the other hand, if you're looking for marketing help, then you'll want to seek out partners that obviously know what they're doing in the market. Perhaps they control the search engine TRAFFIC, perhaps they have a high-ranking product, or perhaps they have a busy forum.

Here's where to find these potential partners:

SEARCH for partners:

- Search for your niche keywords in the search engines. Who controls the organic search engine TRAFFIC for the most competitive words?

- While you're searching the organic results, look at the sponsored pay per click listing to see who's paying top dollar for top spots on competitive words.

- Search in niche publications to see who's consistently paying for advertising. If they keep paying, they must be doing well.

- Search Amazon.com for your keywords to find expert authors in your niche.

- Search ClickBank.com and look at the top products in each category – those are the best sellers.

- Search for your main niche keywords along with the word "forum" to discover how has busy forum in your niche. The busier and bigger the forum, the bigger the owner's "platform" or audience.

- Likewise, search for your niche keywords followed by "blog" to find busy blogs (check the comments to see if they are, indeed, interactive and busy).

- Search for those who have newsletters in your niche too. When you find them, join them so you can see what sort of content they provide.

ASK for partners:

- Ask your existing partners if they can recommend other partners to you.

- Ask your customers and subscribers about other experts and marketers in your niche.

> *Example: Ask them what other newsletters they subscribe to, what blogs they read, what forums they visit, and what sorts of products they buy. Ask them, in particular, who they trust.*

LOOK for partners:

- Look for partners at niche specific trade shows, seminars, conferences, and similar.

- Finally, don't forget to look for potential partners offline at your local businesses. You can do in-store promotions together, physical mailings, seminars and more.

Day 6:

How to Approach Potential Partners With an Irresistible Offer

Remember this:

You're not the only one contacting the potential JV partners and asking them to work with you.

Indeed, you probably are even NOT the only one TODAY.

Some of the best marketers get dozens of offers by email, postal mail, and phone each week – and that means your offer needs to stand out if you want it to be considered.

How do you do that?

Here are a few suggestions and issues for you to consider…

- **Make your offer extraordinary** by going above the "standard" offers in your niche.

- **Make sure it's clear that your potential partner gets the best end of the deal!** In other words, slant the deal towards your partner. Remember: He doesn't need you as much as you need him.

- **Offer something new.** Don't send the same ol' same ol' "joint venture" offer that is really just an invitation to become your affiliate.

- **Go out of your way to make it easy for your potential partner to accept your offer.** Show him that his participation is minimal but that he can expect maximum reward.

- **Related to the last point where your offer requires very little effort**, you should make sure any offer – especially if this is the first time working with a partner – doesn't require much time either from the potential partner.

- **Copywriting rules apply!** If you're sending out a joint venture proposal by email or postal mail, make absolutely sure that it's oriented towards your reader and packed with benefits. He'll wonder "what's in it for me?" when he starts reading your letter – and your letter needs to answer that… immediately!

- **Go ahead and use social proof in the form of name-dropping.** If you've already secured a few well-known partners, tell other potential partners who they are.

- **Whenever possible, build relationships with partners first BEFORE proposing joint ventures.** Your potential JV partners are much more likely to say yes to any request if they already know you.

  After all, most people would choose to work with a friend first, then an acquaintance, with strangers on the bottom of the list. If you take yourself out of the "stranger" category, you'll do better.

- **Ask your current partners for introductions to potential future partners.** Doing so takes you out of the "stranger" category and into the "mutual acquaintance" category.

Now that you know where to find potential partners and how to approach them, there's another question you're likely asking.

Namely, what sort of joint venture can you do together? The answer is simple:

Anything that provides mutual benefit for you and your partners.

That includes but is in no way limited to:

- **Standard affiliate partner arrangements** where one partner promotes the other partner's product or service in exchange for a commission.

- **100% commission arrangements** where one partner promotes the other partner's product for 100% of the profits. In exchange, the product creator is building a mailing list and a customer list from all the TRAFFIC.

- **Link exchanges** on your regular site, your blog, your forum, etc.

- **Exchanging testimonials** on each other's products (provided both products are worthy of good testimonials).

- **Swapping endorsements** in each other's newsletter.

- **Putting each other's links on the other person's subscription confirmation page or product thank you pages**.

- **Swapping articles** to post on each other's sites.

- **Taking turns being guest bloggers** on each other's blogs.

- **Creating a product** together.

- **Doing a postal mailing** together.

- **Giving discount coupons** that can only be used by the partner's customers and subscribers.

  …and so on.

The possibilities are endless – online and offline!

Day 7:
How to Create an Affiliate Program that Attracts Super Affiliates

Just like your in-demand joint venture partners, your in-demand "super" affiliates have plenty of offers on the table. Indeed, they never have to look for things to promote, because people are banging down their doors asking them to promote their products!

As such, the best way to attract super affiliates is to treat them like joint venture partners. That means –

**Make them a <u>special</u> offer they can't refuse and
then approach them INDIVIDUALLY with your offer.**

Here are a few ideas to catch the eyes of the super affiliates...

<u>GIVE</u> more to your super affiliates:

- Give special high commission rates to super affiliates. That means you shouldn't be offering the standard 50% on ebooks, or any other rate that you offer to the rest of your affiliates. Instead, offer upwards of 60% or 75%. You may even consider offering 100% for list-building purposes.

- Give an incentive to promote now, such as a special high commission that lasts for one or two weeks (and then reverts to a special commission rate that isn't quite as high).

Example: you may offer a 90% commission rate for two weeks that reverts to the 75% rate after that period.

ENCOURAGE your super affiliates:

- Encourage super affiliates to continue promoting by offering bonus incentives that kick in after he or she makes so many paid referrals.

- Encourage affiliates to continue promoting by offering things like daily commissions. Again, this should be a special offer. While most affiliates have to wait the traditional 30 days, you can pay super affiliates daily… right into their PayPal account.

OFFER special extras your super affiliates:

- Offer special, unique landing pages for your best affiliates. These landing pages may address the visitors as a group.

Example: "Welcome to Kit Elliott's Newsletter!" This special landing page may include some of the specials listed below.

- Offer contests with big prizes from time to time. Sometimes the biggest super affiliates don't need the money – but a contest kicks in their competitive spirit. You should post a daily leader board on an affiliate contest blog to keep everyone motivated.

- Offer semi-exclusive promotions. For example, offer a handful of your best affiliates the chance to promote a new product a few days before everyone else.

Making a good offer is NOT all about making the affiliate feel special – you should also make a special offer for his or her subscribers. That way the affiliate looks good in the eyes of the readers.

Such specials you might offer include:

- **A special discount rate that's only available to the super affiliate's newsletter subscribers.**
- **A special bonus that's only available to the affiliate's newsletter subscribers.**

Now that you know what to offer super affiliates and other good affiliates, it's time to find them…

Day 8:
Where to Find Super Affiliates

You'll find your super affiliates in the same places that you find potential joint venture partners.

Namely, you may look in:

- Search engines
- Forums
- Blogs
- Newsletters
- Through introductions of other partners
- …and more.

However, here are <u>a few more ways</u> to track down super affiliates…

- **Run a search for the names of the most popular products in your niche**. Which affiliates hold the top organic and pay per click search engine results for those products?

- **Take note of who has busy forums or blogs** – are they also promoting products as an affiliate?

- **Also take note of who is having big product launches with lots of other affiliates**. Often those who use affiliates are also affiliates themselves. And if they have their own successful product, they probably have a good-sized list.

- Depending on what the affiliate link for a particular affiliate program looks like, you may even be able to **run a search to see who all is promoting a particular product**.

- **Post an inquiry about a competitors' products on well-known forums**. Who steps forward to post a review and an affiliate link?

- **Join the affiliate programs of all the known marketers and products in your niche**. Since these marketers may have affiliate contests from time to time, you'll get a sneak peek at the affiliate leader board to see who always does really well.

- **Run a search for the biggest keywords in your niche along with the term "affiliate contest" or "JV blog" or "affiliate blog" and any other similar phrases you can think of**. Doing so will uncover a few affiliate contests blogs – and their leader boards! – that you might not have found on your own.

- **Check out the big article directories** like ezinearticles.com. Who is promoting affiliate products in their articles? Pay particular attention to those whose articles are also ranking well in the search engines.

- **Search for "affiliate directories" in the search engines**. You can post your affiliate program in these directories, of course. But more likely, you will probably find someone who understands affiliate marketing and may be willing to do a mutual endorsement deal.

  While the above ideas will get you a nice list of potential super affiliates, remember that even someone who's never promoted a product before for someone else could be a super affiliate.

> *Example: Some product creators have their own big lists but don't consider themselves as affiliates. Nonetheless, they'd certainly have a responsive audience if you could convince them to promote your product.*

Likewise, look at potential offline partners. They may not be used to being affiliates in the traditional sense, but you most certainly can strike JV-type deals with them.

Day 9:
How to Approach Affiliates

Approaching potential affiliates and especially super affiliates is no different than approaching potential joint venture partners.

That means that –

Ideally you should build a relationship with these potential affiliates first. Ask them what YOU can do FOR THEM.

- If they have a product, promote it first and make money for them.
- If they have a newsletter, become a subscriber so you can better understand this marketer.
- If they go to offline events like seminars, you should go too and introduce yourself.

If building a relationship first isn't possible, then at least **make yourself visible in the niche before approaching potential partners**.

Super affiliates always have their eyes on the products and marketers in their niche – if you make a big "splash" in the niche, they'll notice.

If your product climbs the ClickBank popularity in its category fast, savvy marketers and affiliates will notice.

In other words:

Make a name for yourself first in the niche.

Then when you start looking for people to promote your products, you won't be a stranger.

Next, you'll want to be armed with:

- **Proof**
- **Statistics**
- **Numbers**

…when you approach a potential affiliate.

Remember, he gets lots of offers all the time.

Indeed, the busiest affiliates don't even have time to work with all their friends and acquaintances. That means that –

If you want this person to promote your products, you not only need to make him a good offer, you need to prove that you have a good offer.

The first bit of proof you should give a potential partner is **access to your product.**

Don't even question this one. Just offer free and unlimited access. A good affiliate won't promote something he hasn't seen. And the top affiliates generally don't need to pay out of pocket to get a copy of the product.

If you're asking the person to help you with a launch or some other special promotion on a particular date, then **make sure the product gets into his hands in plenty of time.**

> **Join My Affiliate Program** *If you are an affiliate or would like to earn additional revenue, then, please fill feel free to join my affiliate program at SuperAffiliate.com. We have retired all Web 2.0 properties and moving into a new line of products and services that will convert at a much higher rate!*

You can't expect him to read and promote an offer in the span of a few days.

Two weeks is better – and that's a minimum. Getting the product in his hands a month before launch is better.

That provides proof that your product is good. Now you need to offer **proof that your sales letter is good.**

That is, you want to offer proof that the sales letter converts, which assures the affiliate that he or she can make money with this promotion.

If your product is in a post-launch phase, then it's easy – simple hand over all your stats. You should be able to tell the affiliate your conversion rate across time and across different TRAFFIC sources.

Let him know how many sales he can expect – and multiply that by the commission rate **so he can imagine how much money he'll make.**

If you don't have access to any sales numbers yet (perhaps because you are still in pre-launch), many affiliates will still prefer to get some sort of reassurance that your sales page converts.

For starters, you can give them a sneak preview of the sales page. Good affiliates will be able to spot a bad sales page from miles away. And most of them will get a feel for whether your page converts.

If you have a well-known copywriter creating your sales page, then by all means let the affiliates know this. If you're doing your own copy, tell them how well your most recent product pages have converted. Either way, the affiliates can make an estimate of the conversion rate based on history.

<u>Bottom line:</u> The better offer you can provide, the more the affiliate "knows" you, and the more proof and numbers you can provide, the better chance you have of getting a "yes" from your affiliates.

CHAPTER 3

The "O" in G.R.O.W.I.N.G.

OPTIMIZE Your Site for the Search Engines

In this section of the *G.R.O.W.I.N.G.* formula, you'll learn:

- Day 10: Using on-page optimization to pull in search engine TRAFFIC.

- Day 11: Using off-page optimization tactics to boost your rankings.

- Day 12: How to use the pay per click search engines (like Google AdWords) to drive new subscribers to your site.

Let's start with the regular search engines like Google, Yahoo!, MSN and similar...

Day 10:
Using On-Page Optimization to Pull in Search Engine TRAFFIC

There are basically two steps involved in on-page optimization for your individual web pages:

1) <u>UNCOVER</u> your keywords using special tools.

2) <u>USE</u> on-page optimization tactics to rank well for those keywords.

Here's how to do it…

1) <u>UNCOVER</u> Your Keywords.

Discovering what keywords your market uses to find you is actually fairly easy when you have the right tools. You can use a keyword took like WordTracker. com or use any other keyword tool that you prefer. If you'd like to look at the options, just search for "keyword tool" and you'll find several options (both free and paid) in the search engines.

Once you've selected your tool, start entering some of the more common, broad keywords that describe your niche.

Example: You may enter words like "weight loss," "dog training," "learn to ski," "play piano," "tour Italy," etc.

A good keyword tool will provide you with synonyms and other related words. Then it will create a list of words people in your niche are using to find your products and services – everything from the broad words like "lose weight" to long-tail words like, "how to lose weight over 40."

DEFINED: "Long-Tail Keyword"
A "long-tail keyword" is one that typically
is composed of at least three or more words.
Because it is a longer phrase, it tends to be searched less than a two-word phrase. However, there's also usually less competition in the search engines for these words – meaning you have a good chance of ranking high for that phrase.

> **Quick Tip:** Many keyword tools also give you an idea of how much competition you have in that search engines for that particular word. If your tool doesn't do that, simply plug your keyword into the top search engines (using quotes) and see how many other sites are indexed for that exact keyword.

The keyword tool should give you a good estimate of how often each word is searched per day or per month, so that you can estimate your TRAFFIC if you rank high for that word.

Your goal is to find words that have a decent number of searches per day yet very little competition. While individually your long-tail keywords may not bring in much TRAFFIC, collectively they'll add up to quite a bit of TRAFFIC.

Example: Ranking high for 50 words that each bring in ten visitors means you'll have 500 visitors per day. Unless you're a search engine optimization expert, you'll find it easier to get 500 visitors per day that way as opposed to ranking well for one highly searched yet highly competitive word.

2) _USE_ On-Page Optimization Tactics to Rank for Those Keywords.

Your next step involves sprinkling your keywords throughout the content on your pages, including using your keywords in your navigation menu and other links.

Here are two tips for creating content around keywords:

- **CHOOSE two keyword phrases per page on your site:**

  In other words, don't try to optimize each page for multiple keywords. If you try to optimize for more than a couple, you likely won't rank high for any of them.

- **CREATE content around those keyword phrases:**

  Your next step is to create articles and other content around your keywords. Use your keywords in your article title and in the body of your article.

However, don't "stuff" your page with keywords, as the search engines may decide you're trying to spam them and your page won't rank high if at all.

Instead, use a keyword density rate of about 2% to 3%, meaning your keyword shows up two or three times for every 100 words of content.

While on-page optimization can help you get ranked for some of the less competitive keywords, it can only take you so far.

If you want to rank higher – even for more competitive keywords – you'll need to use off-page optimization strategies too. Here's how…

Day 11:
Using Off-Page Optimization Tactics to Boost Your Rankings

If ranking high for competitive keywords was as easy as optimizing your page for those keywords, anyone could rank high for nearly any keyword.

But those in charge of Google and the other search engines are smart.

They DON'T index and rank pages solely on the content that's on that page. Instead, they look for "votes" from third-party sites. The more "votes" a site gets, and the more votes from high-quality sites, the easier it is for a site to rank high for their keywords.

So how does another site "vote" for your site?

Simple:

By giving your site a one-way incoming link.

You see, Google has devised a system called "Page Rank" (PR) that helps them determine how high to rank your page in their search engine.

The higher your Page Rank, the better your site will rank.

And generally, you increase your page rank by increasing the number of one-way incoming links… especially from sites with high PR.

In other words, all links ("votes") are NOT equal. If you have links coming in a FFA (free for all) link farm that's considered "spammy" by Google, that link won't count much – and indeed, it could even hurt your standings in the search engines.

But get a lot of links coming in from related niche sites with high PR, and you'll see your PR rise… and with it, your rankings for specific keywords.

The second part of getting an incoming link is that the anchor text – which are the words that create the actual link – should be your keywords.

> *Example: If you're trying to rank for "losing weight after pregnancy," then those four words should be the words your link partners use to link to your site.*

How do you get one-way incoming links?

Here are a few places for you to start…

- **SWAP links with other related niche sites.**

  Look for sites that cater to your niche and, preferably, have a high Page Rank. However, don't ignore sites with low Page Rank. If they look like high-quality sites, some day they might have a high PR – in which case you'll benefit.

  Ideally you should get one-way incoming links in order to achieve the most benefit. Usually that means triangulating your sites if you (or your link partner) has more than one site.

> *Example: You link your Site A to your link partner's Site B. Then you partner links his Site B to your Site C. That way all sites have one-way incoming links – and yet you and your link partner effectively swapped reciprocal links.*

- **SUBMIT your sites to relevant directories.**

  One way to get links back to your site is by submitting it to various directories. In particular you should pay attention to niche directories. So if you have a dog site, submit it to dog directories and search engines.

Of course you can submit it to other directories as well, including newsletter directories, blog directories (if you have a blog), forum directories (if you have a forum), local directories and the like.

- **SEND articles to article directories.**

  This is such a great tactic – not only to get backlinks but also to get TRAFFIC – that we'll be talking about it extensively in the "Write Articles" section of this ebook.

Day 12:
Pay Per Click Search Engine Marketing

Pay Per Click (PPC) search engine marketing is just what it sounds like. Rather than paying for your ads to be displayed, you pay only when someone clicks on your ad.

Google AdWords is perhaps the most well-known pay per click search engine, but Yahoo!, MSN and many smaller search engines also offer PPC ads. All of these PPC search engines basically work the same:

The user enters keywords and a list of organic search engine results appear. Alongside those organic results are sponsored ads – those are the PPC ads.

Note: The amount you pay per click depends on how much you bid per keyword. The higher you bid, the higher your ad appears in the results – and the more you pay each time someone clicks on your ad.

Here's how to create a compelling ad that gets clicks in 3 steps:

1) CHOOSE Good Keywords.

If you did your keyword research in Day 10, then you already know what sorts of words your market uses to find you. Now you can

> *Note: The more specific your keywords, the better quality of TRAFFIC you'll have coming into your site!*

take this list of keywords to the PPC search engines like AdWords, plug them in, and get an estimate of how much TRAFFIC you can get from these words and how much you'll need to pay for this TRAFFIC.

If you're just getting started with pay per click advertising, bid on the lower range of bids. That way you can test your ad, your landing page, and your autoresponder series (backend marketing) without spending a fortune.

Example: Someone who's searching for "dog training" could be seeking out any number of topics such as house training, obedience training, hunting dog training, agility training, flyball training, guide dog training... and so on.

If your site teaches hunting dog training and you get people coming in looking for flyball training, you won't have a high conversion rate.

To avoid this, simply bid on very specific keywords.

Example: Choose long-tail keywords that reflect your site such as "how to teach a duck retriever dog."

2) CREATE "Clickable" Ads.

Your next step is create ads that get attention and get clicks.

That means you need to create headlines and short ads that promise benefits and, ideally, arouse curiosity.

As you create your ads remember that all copywriting rules apply.

But also remember this:

Your ad is to get clicks. Period.

You see, some ad writers believe that the purpose of your ad is to sell some-thing to the prospect. But because an ad is only three lines long (one line for the headline and two for the ad itself), there simply isn't enough room to properly sell anything to anybody.

Instead you should use your ad for these purposes:

- **The headline is to get attention. Since you have something free to offer the reader (some freebie or solution to a problem via your newsletter), you may use the trigger word "free" in your headline.**

But again, you don't have to sell anything in your headline. Your headline's sole purpose is to attract attention and get the person to read your short ad.

- **The ad's purpose is to elicit a click through. To do this, your ad should promise a benefit and arouse curiosity.**

Here's an example of a short ad that gets attention and gets clicks:

> **Lose Weight FREE!**
> **Dieting and exercising suck.**
> **Here's a better way to burn fat!**
> **www.yourwebsite.com**

The headline gets the attention of everyone seeking to lose weight, plus it promises something for free.

The second line is unusual in that it uses the word "suck." Although words like that shouldn't be overused, throwing them in from time to time can get attention and hold the reader's interest.

Finally, **the third line** promises a benefit ("a better way to burn fat"), but it also arouses curiosity since it doesn't tell the reader any more details. It leaves the reader thinking, "what's a better way to lose weight than diet and exercise?"

And with a "click" the reader is sent to your landing page…

3) <u>COMPEL</u> the Prospect to Join Your Newsletter.

The final step in using pay per click ads to get TRAFFIC and newsletter subscribers is to create a landing page (squeeze page) that compels visitors to join your newsletter. You've already completed this step. If you need a refresher, just return to "Day 1" of this ebook.

And that's it! That's all there is to growing your list via organic search engine results and pay per click results.

Now it's time to move onto an entirely different strategy, one that the content-lovers and writers will enjoy (and profit from!) immensely…

The "W" in G.R.O.W.I.N.G.
WRITE Articles

The next strategy you can use to get new newsletter subscribers is easy and, if you do it yourself rather than outsourcing, it's also absolutely free.

So what's the strategy? Simple: Writing articles.

When most people think of "writing articles," they think of submitting them to article directories. We'll talk about that in this section since it's important. But there are a whole lot of other things you can do with articles, including using them as content for forum posts, creating videos around them and more.

In this section of the *G.R.O.W.I.N.G.* formula, you'll learn:

- Day 13: How to write a good article.
- Day 14: How to write a resource box that gets clicks.

- Day 15: Submitting your articles to article directories.
- Day 16: Growing your list with blogging.
- Day 17: Posting articles on Web 2.0 content sites.
- Day 18: How to get TRAFFIC using articles and Yahoo! Answers.
- Day 19: How to build your list using articles and forum marketing.
- Day 20: How to use video marketing to grow your list.

Your first step, of course, is to write a good article that serves its purpose. That's where we'll start on lucky number Day 13…

Day 13:
How to Write a Good Article

Anyone can write an article. The trick is to write an article that's engaging enough to attract attention and get read from top to bottom… all the way down to your byline that links to your site. That's your goal – and that's what we're discussing in this section in these three steps:

1) SIZZLING titles.

2) SENSATIONAL articles.

3) SEARCH ENGINE bait.

Let's start with your title…

1) *SIZZLING* Titles

OK, so an article isn't the same thing as an advertisement. But nonetheless, using the copywriting rules you've learned will help you write better articles. In particular, this applies to creating headlines for your articles.

Just like your ad and landing page headlines, your article headlines will benefit from promising a benefit and/or arousing curiosity. Your headlines will also benefit from using trigger words like "how to," "easy" and "discover."

Remember this:

**People want solutions to their problems.
But they also want these solutions to
be quick and easy.**

As such, make sure your headline (title) doesn't make the solution sound like it's a lot of work.

Example: A headline like "The Quick and Easy Way to Lose Weight" will go over much better than "Losing Weight Requires Sacrifice and a Growling Stomach."

People also like to read articles that organized into quick and easy STEPS or TIPS.

That means creating a headline that says something like: "Three Quick and Easy Steps to Losing Weight" or "How to Housetrain Your Puppy in Seven Steps" make for good titles.

When creating titles, remember the purpose of your title.

Simply, the title's purpose is to get attention and draw people into the article.

Go ahead and play with a few different titles. Take some time to create them – after all, it IS the most important part of your article! Without a good title, the article simply won't get read!

2) *SENSATIONAL* Articles

If your article title did a good job, then you've grabbed the eager reader's attention and pulled him into your article. Now your article needs to hold his attention so he reads all the way through to your byline.

Here are a few tips to accomplish exactly that:

- **Write with a conversational tone.**

This isn't a college thesis – and it shouldn't read like one either. Instead of writing as if you're writing a paper for your high school English teacher, write as if you were explaining something to an acquaintance.

- **Make it easy to read…**

If you heeded the first tip, then chances are your article is easy to read. That means you're not using "one hundred dollar" words or bloated sentences. Doing so slows the reader down and may even make him reconsider reading your article at all.

- **…And make it LOOK easy to read!**

In addition to making it easy to read, you also need to format so it LOOKS easy to read. If the reader scans down the article to see long, unbroken blocks of text, he'll likely move on because the article looks difficult to read.

Your first paragraph in particular should be short – indeed, one short sentence to "hook" the reader. Thereafter, every paragraph should only be a few lines long.

Whenever possible, break your text up into interesting segment. For example, create bold sub-headlines that break up the text. Set tips apart from the regular flow of the text. Use numbered or bullets to create lists (as opposed to creating lists within paragraphs).

Once you've completed your article, scan down the article without reading the text. Does the format make the article look easy to read? If not, rewrite and reformat until you have an article that can be quickly consumed.

• Don't Solve Your Readers' Problems Completely!

Your article should help your readers solve a problem – but you don't want to solve it completely! After all, if you give the reader all the information she needs, then she has no reason to click through to your site.

So create an article that's entertaining, useful, and partially solves a problem – but purposely leave the best information off so you can direct your readers to your site for the full solution.

Example: Your weight loss article may give several weight-loss tips. However, you can hold back one of your BEST tips and offer it only to those who click through to your site and subscribe to your newsletter.

3) *SEARCH ENGINE* Bait

Sometimes you'll create articles for your newsletter subscribers as a means of building a relationship and turning them into buyers. However, what we're specifically talking about in this section is using articles to pull in TRAFFIC – and in some cases, that means pulling in search engine TRAFFIC.

You've already learned how to research long-tail keywords and create articles around these keywords. For a refresher, just refer back to Day 10.

Day 14:

How to Write a Resource Box That Gets Clicks

Your "resource boc," which is also known as the "byline," "author's box," and similar names, appears at the end of your article. As mentioned –

The entire goal of your article is to get people to readall the way down to your resource box... and then CLICK on it.

Many beginning marketers completely waste this valuable real estate. Instead of giving their readers a reason to click on their links, they instead talk about themselves.

I'm sure you've seen this many times before.

How many times have you encountered a resource box that goes something like this:

"John Doe is a certified personal trainer with ten years of experience…"

I didn't even bother creating the rest of that fictional resource box because hardly anyone would read it anyway.

And here's why:

Your reader doesn't care about you.

He doesn't care if you're certified in anything, if you have X number of years experience, if you graduated with this degree from that college, etc. And so insisting on talking about yourself and your accomplishments will result in a quick click of the "back button" by a bored-to-tears reader.

The only thing your reader cares about is himself.

That's it!

He only cares about his problems and how you can solve them. If you list anything about yourself, you better directly tie it into a benefit for him.

Otherwise, leave it off and make sure your ad is entirely about what benefits him (the reader).

Notice I used the word "ad" in the above sentence. <u>That's no accident</u>. Your resource box isn't an author biography, even if that's how some people use it.

No, your resource box is an advertisement that gives readers a clear and compelling reason for them to click through to your site. And like every other ad we've talked about in this ebook, that usually means offering a benefit and perhaps arousing curiosity.

But here's the good news:

You can be somewhat of a mind reader with regards to your prospects, thus increasing your conversion rate. That's because you already know what has caught the attention of your prospect – if they read your article, then **offering them more of the same (but even better!) is a sure way to get them to click through!**

Indeed, you can even offer them more of the same by asking them to click through for "Part 2" of the article. Or, as mentioned previously, you can offer a free ebook that's an extension of the article with some of your best tips inside.

66

Quick Tip:

As always, take the time to segment your list. If someone is reading an article about "lifting weights to lose weight," then don't send them to the same landing page as the person who's reading your article about, "diet pills that work almost like magic."

While there might be some overlap between the markets reading those articles, chances are you're talking about different niches. If you keep them on separate lists – or at least segment your list so you can separate out these niches – then you can target your lists better and send emails that speak directly to the different niches.

And as always, that means more sales and more money for you!

99

Summary and Action Steps

Now that you have a good idea how to create an engaging article and a compelling resource box, it's time for you to crank a few articles out.

1. Block aside an entire day and see if you can create at least ten articles

that range anywhere from 350 words to about 700 words.

2. Then set aside time every week to write articles.

Or if you don't want to do it yourself, then hire a ghostwriter to create these articles for you.

You're probably wondering how many you should write per week.

That depends (in part) on how much this content strategy plays into your overall marketing plan. Since it's likely that you'll need a lot of content since you'll be using article marketing plus blogging and writing articles for your newsletter, you should plan on writing at least ten per week.

Of course this is one of those cases where **the more you can do, the better.**

If you can create 25 articles per week – 100 per month – then go for it. They'll pay out quickly in terms of TRAFFIC, list building and sales… and you're also likely to see a long-term pay out as well.

On the other hand, don't scrap article marketing if you don't have the time or money to create a large number of articles.

Consider this: If you can only create just one article per week, that's 52 articles per year. And that will bring you in money and TRAFFIC. So is it worth it? You bet!

Day 15:

Submit Your Articles to Article Directories

One of the most common ways to market your site with articles is by submitting those articles to article directories.

- Sometimes publishers pick them up and reprint them, meaning you get an influx of TRAFFIC.
- Other times submitting to these directories is beneficial for search engine TRAFFIC.

If you plan on using your articles for these purposes, then –

You should definitely be creating articles around your "long tail keywords."

Many of these directories are viewed favorably by the search engines, so you may rank well for those keywords simply by submitting to these sites.

In addition to pulling in search engine TRAFFIC indirectly, submitting to article directories is an easy way for you to get one-way incoming links from reputable sites.

How Should You Submit Articles? Some people focus on a handful of the best directories, as they've found these sites get them the best TRAFFIC and the most benefit in terms of links. In this case, it doesn't take but a few minutes to submit your articles to the directories.

Other people outsource their article writing to ghostwriters who are willing to include article submission as part of their fee. Even if you're writing your own articles, you can still hire someone to submit them for you if you find it a time-consuming task.

Finally, those who mass submit to many directories sometimes choose to use software designed for this purpose. Simply search for "article submission software" to uncover a few options. Most of this software offers free trials or partial submissions for free just so you can try the service first before buying.

In this section we'll list several of the more well-known sites. If you venture out on your own to uncover other article directories, do your due diligence first to ensure it is, indeed, considered a reputable directory.

Here are five of the more well-known article directories – in alphabetical order:

- **ArticleCity.com**
- **ArticleSnatch.com**
- **Buzzle.com**
- **EzineArticles.com**
- **GoArticles.com**

If you get started with these seven you'll likely find your site getting plenty of TRAFFIC – and your newsletter getting plenty of new subscribers!

For loads more, simply run a search in Google or your favorite search engine for "article directory." You may also search for niche-specific article directories in the search engines.

Quick Tip: If your time is so limited on any particular day that you can only submit to one directory, start with EzineArticles.com.

As you begin submitting to directories more often, you'll get a sense for which ones provide you the most benefits – then you can focus on those that are best for your niche and your TRAFFIC.

Day 16:
Grow Your List with Blogging

The second way you can use articles to grow your list is by posting them on your blog.

At this point many marketers ask the question:

How long should the article be?

The length you ultimately choose for blog posts should be as unique as your blog.

- Some people tend to post 200 or 300 word articles – just tips and snippets of information… but they post regularly.

- Others post full-length "average" size articles around 400 to 600 words.

- Still others post long articles (even as long as 1000 words or so).

Experiment a little to find out what works for you.

Chances are, you'll find that posting a mix of articles will serve you well.

Now let's look at some of the amazing ways you can benefit by posting articles on your blog…

1. Search engine TRAFFIC: Keyword-optimized articles placed on your blogs can attract search engine TRAFFIC.

And since we've talked about search engine TRAFFIC so much throughout this ebook, you know how powerful this TRAFFIC is. Many of these visitors are looking for information – and so it's often easy to convert these visitors to subscribers… and buyers.

2. _Stickiness_: A regularly updated blog makes your site "sticky."

That means visitors tend to return again and again to see what's new on your site. You may find this particularly true when you allow comments on your site, which allows your growing community to enjoy interactive discussions on your blog.

3. _Secure backlinks_: If you run a good blog with thoughtful posts, you'll find other bloggers giving you backlinks.

Experiment a little to find out what sorts of posts get you the most buzz or the most links. For example, if you're the first to report on some bit of news in your niche – and you report thoughtfully – you can expect others to link to your original article and post their own comments.

Another way to get people talking is to make controversial posts from time to time. Other bloggers will take sides – and whether they take your side of the issue or not, they'll link to your blog to discuss your post.

4. _Secret blog posts build lists!_ Some regular visitors will appreciate if you notify them every time you make a new post on your blog.

In other words, you can build a list solely from those wanting to be notified of new blog posts.

But here's an even better inside tip…

From time to time, you should post "top secret" articles on your site that are only accessible using a password. Those who are on your notify list will automatically receive the password. Those who find the post through other means are told they need to join your newsletter list in order to get access to the secret posts!

People love secrets… and so that means loads of new subscribers to your newsletter!

Professional Blog Themes: You should use a professional theme from WooThemes. I have switched to WooThemes for all of my websites after spending thousands on customization and design. WooThemes comes equipped with a built-in customization dash board that saves you a lot of time and money on programming and design. Take a look at KitElliott.com.

> " *Quick Tip: Of course in order to get these new subscribers, you need to "tease" them a bit with the secret blog posts. Give them a taste of the post to build their curiosity and anticipation – then leave them with the option to join the newsletter list to get the password.* "

If you click on the "WooThemes" logo in the lower right corner of KitElliott. com – you will be taken to a list of all of the professional themes that I use. I get credit for any referrals from this link!

Day 17:
Post Articles on Web 2.0 Content Sites

Another way for you to use your articles to drive targeted TRAFFIC to your site (and subscribers to your newsletter) is by using your article content to create focused one-page websites on Squidoo.com and HubPages.com.

What are these sites? Basically, Squidoo and HubPages are Web 2.0 content sites that allow users (like you) to create information pages on nearly any topic, especially if it's a family friendly topic.

So why would you want to even bother creating a web page on someone else's site?

Simple:

Because these sites are like article directories on steroids.

Not only can you optimize your page for a couple different keywords, you're likely to find that you rank HIGH for those keywords. That's because Google absolutely loves HubPages and Squidoo! (And of course you get the benefits of having one-way incoming backlinks, too.)

There are other benefits of creating article-driven content pages on these sites, too…

> **Interactivity:** Both Squidoo and HubPages allow you to create interactive sites, which means you'll get visitors coming back again and again. Specifically, you can post interactive polls, make blog posts that allow comments, and similar.

Multimedia: You can also easily add multimedia modules to your pages such as videos from various sources, audio, etc.

While the TRAFFIC coming in from the search engines is nice, you're also likely to get plenty of TRAFFIC from people directly visiting Squidoo or HubPages. And all of that adds up to plenty of visitors and lots of repeat visitors.

Your job, of course, is to translate these visitors to newsletter subscribers.

It's relatively easily to do on Squidoo and HubPages, as both of them allow you to link back multiple times to your own site. That means you can have multiple short "advertisements" on your Squidoo lens or HubPage that give readers a compelling reason to click through to your site... and sign up for your newsletter.

<u>Quick Tip</u>: Refer back to Day 1 for tips on creating a good landing page. See also Day 14 for a reminder of how to write a good ad (resource box) at the end of your articles.

So what's the catch?

In order to have your page accepted on Squidoo and HubPages and ranked highly in their internal search engines and "top pages" lists, **you need to meet their editorial guidelines**.

They're not difficult to follow, but you should read the terms of service to make sure your site doesn't violate any of their policies.

Example: HubPages really prefers that you only have two links going back to one site.

The second "catch" is that in order to get TRAFFIC from Squidoo and Hub-Pages visitors directly, **you need to get your pages ranked highly internally.** And to do that, you need to do things like drive TRAFFIC to your page, get others to rank your lens or Module highly and similar.

In other words –

> ### You need to spend some time creating a useful page full of content that others will enjoy, and you need to spend some time building TRAFFIC to this site.

While both of these sites do provide good TRAFFIC and high quality back links, you shouldn't be promoting your Squidoo lens or HubPages to the exclusion of working on pages on your own domain.

That is, **you should be building your OWN site and sending TRAFFIC to your own site FIRST.**

Then, time permitting; you can work on creating Squidoo lenses and Hub-Pages.

Day 18:
How to Get TRAFFIC Using Articles and Yahoo! Answers

Another way for you to drive TRAFFIC to your site and get newsletter sub-scribers is by using articles to answer questions on Yahoo! Answers.

If you prefer, you can of course simply type in new answers every time you see a question related to your niche.

However, as time goes by you're likely to see the same questions pop up again and again.

You can make it easy on yourself by copying and pasting a well-written article as your answer.

Here's how to make the most out of posting on Yahoo! Answers…

GET involved in the social aspect of the site.

Yahoo! Answers allows you to set up a profile and build a network of fans and friends on the site. If you intend to use Yahoo! Answers regularly, then you should definitely use this feature. Doing so makes you more familiar to others on the site and positions you as an expert in your niche.

GO to the site multiple times during the day.

There are two main ways to find questions to answer on the site.

One way is to <u>search for your niche related keywords</u>. This doesn't tend to be a very good method, as the site currently doesn't let you sort questions by date (or time) posted.

The second way is to <u>visit the appropriate category</u> and browse for questions in your niche. This is a better method, as questions are displayed with the most recent questions on top. Since you want to answer as many questions as you can when they're first posted, it's a good idea to check the site periodically during the day.

GROW your mailing list by citing your website as the source of your information.

Yahoo! Answers allows you to post links to whatever source you used to answer your question. Naturally, you'll want to post links to your own site.

However, you should be cautious when doing so. Do NOT "plug" your site in a hyped up, commercial way. Instead, leave your link as the source of your info, and include a note about how even more information can be found on your site.

Yes, you're still giving people a reason to click through to your site to join your newsletter – but you're not being quite so brazen about it.

GIVE generously and post thoughtfully.

The better answers you post on Yahoo! Answers, the more likely it is that people will rate your answers highly. It also greatly increases the chances that your answer will be chosen as the best answer – and that's a good thing, because once the question is closed, your answer (and your link!) will appear just under the question.

In Summary: Using Yahoo! Articles is not only a way to get backlinks and drive TRAFFIC to your site; it's also a way to establish yourself as an expert in your niche. That means that the more you post, the more TRAFFIC you can expect to receive. And the more TRAFFIC you get, the bigger (and faster) your list grows!

Day 19:
How to Build Your List Using Articles and Forum Marketing

Just as with Yahoo! Answers, we've grouped forum marketing under the broader category of "article marketing." However, you do NOT have to use articles to participate in forums. Just use the participation and promotion tips below while disregarding any specific mention of the articles themselves.

If you do use articles, then there are two approaches you can use:

1. <u>POST</u> articles outright on forums, being sure to include your signature link at the bottom of your post.

If you're interested in this method, read the terms of service of the forum first and spend some time lurking to find out if this is allowed.

Some forums have place right on the forum where you can post articles. Others allow you to post articles for discussion. But others frown on members posting articles and will delete your post since articles can easily look "spammy" on a discussion forum.

2. <u>PREPARE</u> articles based on frequently asked questions (FAQs) and post these articles whenever someone asks one of these FAQs.

This is similar to the method discussed on Day 18 where you create articles based on questions you often see asked. Basically, it just saves you time to create these articles as opposed to creating a new post every time someone asks that same question.

So how do you make the most of your forum participation and promotions? The idea is to:

- Participate thoughtfully, first…

- And ONLY THEN drop your signature link (a small ad and link back to your site) at the end of your post.

Here are a few tips to get you started…

- SEEK forums in your niche.

  One of the easiest ways to find forums in your niche is to use Google or your favorite search engine. Simply enter your niche's keywords alongside the word "forum" or "discussion" or "message board."

Also, be sure to check out the well-known marketers' sites in your niche, as many of them have busy forums.

- **SIFT THROUGH the terms of service and policies.**

Before you do anything, sift through and read the terms of service on the forums you're interested in. Some forums, for example, do not allow signature links (also known as "sig links"). That's the type of forum you'll likely want to pass on in favor of forums that encourage sig links.

- **SIGN UP for an account.**

When you find forums whose terms of service are agreeable to your philosophy on forum participation, sign up immediately for an account. That's because you want to start "aging" your account immediately. Many people look favorably upon people who have been members of a forum for quite some time.

- **SPEND some time lurking.**

Don't start posting immediately. Instead, spend some time "lurking" (reading but not posting) to get a feel for the "flavor" of the community. You'll get a sense of the unwritten rules of the forum, the rhythm of the forum and you'll be able to get to know some of the key players on the forum.

- **START posting thoughtfully.**

Once you have a good handle on how this particular forum works, you can start posting thoughtfully. You may want to start with an introduction post. Then move on to answering questions.

Spend about a week posting good answers to build your credibility and establish yourself as an expert in the niche. Then, once you have a few good posts under your belt…

- **SLIP your signature link at the end of your posts.**

  Once you've started building your reputation on the forum (and people don't think you're just blowing through to drop a signature link), then you can, indeed, start leaving your signature link at the end of your posts.

How do you create a good signature link?

Some people just leave a link at the end of their posts, with a title along the lines of "my website" or "my newsletter."

Sure, a few people might click through to view the website or sign up for the newsletter. But that number is going to be small. And that's because the signature line provides absolutely no reason for the forum visitor to click through.

Your signature line is like your article resource box – **it's a small ad and a link that's ALL about the reader**.

It's NOT about you.

It's about the reader's problems and how you can solve them. As such, the signature line should always give the reader a good, compelling reason why she should click on the link.

<u>Note</u>: For a refresher on how to create this sort of small ad, refer back to Day 14.

Day 20:

How to Use Video Marketing to Grow Your List

You've probably noticed video is "hot" right now.

Just look at the popularity and success of video sites like YouTube. And if you spend any time on these video uploading sites, you'll notice they're not all videos of cats and dogs doing funny things.

Indeed, **many marketers are taking advantage of this medium to <u>sell their products</u> and <u>grow their lists</u>**.

Can you get in on a piece of this action? You bet.

> <u>Note</u>: Again, these tactics falls under the broader category of "article marketing." While you can use create and distribute article videos to grow your list, you can also create videos without the use of articles. If you choose that route, follow the tips below while disregarding references to articles.

First off, however, you need to consider your market. Are they on high speed connections that can easily handle video?

> *Example: If you're catering to a rural market, they simply may not be capable of a true broadband connection.*

If you're certain that your market is capable of watching videos, then you'll want to start experimenting with them to see how they can help your business.

There are a few different ways to use videos with respects to growing your list.

One way is to **offer a free video or two as your freebie for anyone who signs up for your list.**

Another way is to **use your videos as "bait" to attract prospects to your site.** This works much the same way as article marketing – you create impressive content with a call to action at the end that asks people to visit your site. People click through to your site and land on your compelling squeeze page.

> **Quick Tip**: If people want to join your list after watching one of your videos, then offering "more of the same" is a good tactic to increase your subscriber opt-in rate. In other words, you can offer a video as your bonus freebie for joining your newsletter list.

Let's talk about creating videos that get buzz… and new subscribers.

Here are the three steps to creating and launching a buzz-worthy video…

1. *BUY good video and audio equipment.*

Some people say – and it might be true – that prospects who are hungry for a particular piece of information wouldn't care if you wrote it down on a piece of toilet paper.

> **Quick Tip**: Let's suppose I gave you the winning lottery numbers for tomorrow's lottery. Would you care whether I scratched it on the back of a napkin or engraved it on a bar of gold? Probably not.

But of course we're not all creating products that are the equivalent to a set of winning lottery numbers. So for the rest of us, **presentation counts**. That means you should buy the best video, audio and lighting equipment you can afford in order to create the most professional, polished videos you can muster.

2. <u>BE</u> creative… and controversial!

Prospects may appreciate plain, straightforward information – but they'll rarely pass those sorts of videos along to their friends, post links to your video in forums, or blog about them.

If you want to create videos that get talked about, then they need to be centered around content that pushes the envelope. Be creative. Be controversial. Maybe even be a little offensive. After all, polarizing people and creating controversy results in plenty of niche buzz!

<u>Quick Tip</u>: Remember, your video has purpose. Namely, you're using it to bring people to your site to join your newsletter. Always keep that overriding purpose in mind as you produce your video.

Also, be sure to include your link multiple times throughout the video in both text and verbal form… especially at the end of the video. And as always, be sure to give those who view your video a compelling reason to go to your site!

3. <u>BEGIN</u> your video launch with a BANG!

Once you've completed your video, it's time to get it in front of as many people as possible. If you can launch it with a "bang" – and if it truly is a viral video – then you can expect it to soon take on a life of it's own.

For starters, post your video on the following sites and places:

- Upload your video to <u>YouTube</u>, <u>Yahoo! Video</u>, <u>Viddler.com</u> and as many other video sites as you can.
- Post links to your video on your <u>Squidoo</u> lens and <u>HubPages</u>.

- Post links to your video on your blog, website, and forum.

- Post links to your video on other niche forums. (If nothing else, post it in your sig line.)

- Announce your video to your list, and encourage them to pass it along to their friends.

- Ask your friends and colleagues to blog about your video as well as adding it to their <u>Squidoo</u> lenses, <u>HubPages</u>, forums, newsletter and similar.

- Submit articles to article directories and include a link to your video at the end of the article.

- And finally: If your video is considered controversial or even offensive, then be sure to get it into the hands of the people who will be the most offended by the content. These people WILL talk about it, post links on forums, and blog about it too!

Talking about viral videos leads us directly into our next main topic.

Indeed, on Day 27 we'll talk about even more strategies to help your video go viral.

CHAPTER 5

The "I" in G.R.O.W.I.N.G.

INVITE Others to Spread Your Marketing Messages

Inviting – or incentivizing – your market to spread your marketing message is the definition of viral marketing.

When your marketing "goes viral," it means –

It's taken on a life of its own, it's buzz worthy, and everyone in your niche is talking about it or using something you've created.

There are plenty of ways to do create viral tools, products and reports. One way to do it (as discussed on Day 20) is to create content that's controversial, polarizing, useful, engaging or perhaps even a little offensive.

Example: For an example of how this works in the real world, just look at some of the "shock jocks" and other U.S. personalities such as political commentator Ann Coulter, shock jocks Howard Stern and Don Imus, and many others.

These are people who make a living saying controversial and even downright offensive things. When they do, their fans applaud and spread their controversial or offensive video clips or writing around.

Likewise, there's always a group that's completely offended – and they too spread the video clips and writings around, if only to discuss just the offensiveness of the particular piece.

Of course you don't have to create something controversial or offensive.

Sometimes humor gets spread around. Just think of how often someone has passed along a funny email, joke, or YouTube video clip to you.

You can also create tools and software with your marketing message embedded.

Example: Free email companies like Hotmail exploded on the scene and went viral immediately. That's because everyone who uses their email service ALSO passes along their marketing message, as Hotmail and others include a little ad at the bottom of each email they send out.

You probably don't want to offer free email to your users, but there are other tools you can give prospects with your marketing message embedded.

Example: If your market includes a lot of bloggers, then you can offer free blog themes with your link at the bottom.

Since you're likely an information marketer, for our purposes we're going to focus on creating viral information products in this section.

In this section of the *G.R.O.W.I.N.G.* formula, you'll learn:

- Day 21: How to kick start your viral marketing.
- Day 22: Using contest giveaways to grow your list.
- Day 23: How to use JV giveaways to grow your list fast.
- Day 24: How to use quizzes to build your list.
- Day 25: Using petitions to create viral TRAFFIC and build your list.
- Day 26: How to create ebooks and reports that go viral.
- Day 27: How to create videos that go viral.
- Day 28: How to create tools and other content that goes viral.

And first, let's talk about giving your viral products a "boost" to get them going…

Day 21:
How to Kick Start Your Viral Marketing

If you create a video, report or other product that you hope will go viral, then you need to kick start it by initially **getting it into as many of your prospects' hands** as possible.

To do otherwise means your efforts will start with a whimper rather than a bang.

Can a product go viral even if it's not released using a carefully thought-out launch plan?

Of course. But the viral effect will be all the more greater – like a snowball rolling down a hill and gather speed and size – if you actually launch the video, report or other free product.

In short:

You need to market your viral product to get it in front of your audience!

Throughout this section, we'll discuss specific tips and tactics for getting your product out to your prospects.

But first, let's look at who needs to get their hands on your viral product immediately…

1. _GET_ your viral product into your _prospects'_ hands.

This one is obvious – and this is the one we'll talk about most in this section.

2. _GIVE_ your viral product to your _affiliates_ and _joint venture partners_.

This is the one that many marketers new to viral marketing overlook. The reason is because they assume that a product mainly goes viral because the prospects propel it forward. However, having affiliates and joint venture partners help you launch it gets it in front of more prospects… which kick starts the whole viral process.

Your **action step** for this day is easy.

All you have to do is draw up two lists:

1. On the first list, **write down all the ways you can market your free viral product.**

    In other words, you're asking yourself where your

target market hangs out – and how you can get in front of them.

2. Second, **draw up a list of potential affiliates and joint venture marketing partners.**

   If you're not in regular contact with these people, then get in contact with them to start building a relationship. Otherwise, polish of your joint venture proposal letter in preparation for asking them to help you launch your viral product.

Now let's look at specific viral products and events you can use to build your list…

Day 22:
Using Contest Giveaways to Grow Your List

One way to grow your list quickly is to <u>hold a contest</u>.

Here's why it works:

In order for people to participate in the contest and have a shot at winning a prize, they need to opt-in to your newsletter list. And because everyone loves to enter contests, it's one of those things where people tend to tell their friends.

Example: Don't count on people to think of telling their friends. Instead, you should actually encourage them to do so! Using a Tell-A-Friend (TAF) form can also help with the viral effect.

But there's also a potential problem…

If you think back to what we talked about on Day 4 (how to avoid freebie seekers from flooding your list), you can see that this is one of those tactics that has the potential to attract people who are unwilling or unable to buy your product.

You can get around that potential problem by following these tips…

- **Make sure your contest prizes appeal to your target market.**

    One way to bring freebie seekers out of the woodwork is to offer "general interest" prizes. If you do that, then you'll end up with a list of people who aren't all that interested in your niche products and services.

    Example: Let's suppose you're running a dog training site. If you decide to run a contest, then ideally you should offer dog-training related prizes. Whatever you do, don't offer things like cash, iPods, gift certificates to restaurants and similar.

So what, exactly, should you offer up for prizes?

- **Ideally, offer your own products and services as prizes.**

    Makes sense, right? That way the only people who enter your contest are those that are interested in your niche-specific products.

    Of course, a freebie seeker who's interested in your niche is likely to still enter your contest. But that's better than having a list full of freebie seekers who aren't even interested in your niche.

And besides, having freebie seekers who are interested in your niche can actually be beneficial. Even though they might not buy your product, they can still participate in the viral effect by telling OTHERS about your contest.

- **Post your contest offer selectively.**

  You'll want to advertise your contest on niche-specific forums, blogs and other sites. Try to avoid the general "contest" sites, as those types of forums are brimming with freebie seekers.

- **Everyone should "win" your contest.**

  You've likely set up your contest so that you have a grand-prize winner and several "runners up" who win lesser prizes. But if you'd like to make some fast sales, everyone who participates in the contest should get a "prize." And that prize, specifically, should be a limited-time but very generous discount on your products.

A Tip to Make More Sales After the Contest

You may be tempted to run a regular "random drawing" contest. However, you're likely to make a lot more money if you create a contest that centers around contestant participation and, in particular, getting the contestants to "sell" themselves on your product.

After all, much of our marketing activities center around persuasion. We spend hours of our time and thousands of dollars creating sales letters, follow up emails, and squeeze pages, upsells and other sales pieces.

- **So what better way to sell something to someone than to have them persuade themselves to buy?**

And that's exactly what you can do if you set up your contest right.

> Example: Your contestants may be required to write a one or two page "essay" on why your product is right for them, what are the best benefits of your product and so on.

When the contest ends, you'll have many people on your hands who are ready to buy because they've convinced themselves that your product absolutely rocks.

And that's when you offer them the "consolation prize" of a limited-time discount… and then sit back to watch the sales roll in!

Day 23:
How to Use JV Giveaways to Grow Your List Fast

Here's another fast way to add hundreds or even thousands of new subscribers to your list, fast.

Namely, by participating in a niche-specific JV (joint venture) giveaway event.

Here's how it works…

A group of marketers in the same niche get together for a giveaway event. Each marketer offers something of value to add to the event.

These don't tend to be small events with a handful of marketers contributing products. Rather you'll more likely see at least half a dozen to several dozen marketers chipping in products for the event.

Now here's why you're able to build your list…

The <u>only way</u> someone can get their hands on your freebie is by opting into your newsletter list.

You can also see why **you should be offering something valuable** – when a giveaway event visitor is faced with opting into a dozen or more lists to receive freebies, he's likely to pick and choose carefully so he only requests the freebies he really wants.

That means if you create a super-attractive freebie AND give visitors a compelling reason why they should opt in (to yet another list!) to get your freebie, you can expect plenty of new subscribers.

The final component that pulls the entire event together to make it a success is that **all the participating marketers tell their lists about the event, blog about the event, and so on**.

> *Note: Giving something of value means you should create something entirely new for this event, or you should be giving away something that you previously sold. Either way, just make sure you aren't giving away a freebie that you've given away elsewhere.*
>
> *If everyone gives away valuable products, the giveaway event itself earns a good reputation.*

Usually, event participants are given a special link to promote the event. That way the event organizers can offer "perks" to those who send lots of TRAFFIC, such as showing the marketer's freebie at the top of the list (which means that marketer will get more new subscribers).

These events are viral because not only do you have several marketers telling their lists about them, you also have the prospects talking about the event.

Do Giveaway Events Work?

Yes, giveaway events DO work… meaning you can <u>build your list very quickly</u>.

However, the downside is that some of these giveaway events attract freebie seekers.

As such, you'll need to select your giveaway item carefully so that it's most attractive to your niche market.

You'll also need to have a **special autoresponder series in place to help build a relationship with your new subscribers**.

> ## Quick Tip:
>
> One of the first things you should pitch to your new "giveaway event" subscribers is a relatively cheap product – something in the range of $10. That's a "no brainer" price, meaning you should have high conversions if your product is in demand and the copy is persuasive.
>
> Offering these low-priced products up front is one way to get subscribers to take the plunge and make that first purchase with you. Once they've done that, you have them in your sales funnel – which makes it easier for you to sell more products and more expensive products to these new customers.

Day 24:
How to Use Quizzes to Build Your List

Here's a fun one that may not work for every niche. But if you can use it to attract your target market, you may see a huge viral effect.

Quizzes are huge in certain circles.

Open up almost any women's magazine, and you're likely to see at least one quiz. Women take these quizzes to find out if their boyfriends are compatible, what sort of friend they are, and everything and anything else you can think of.

Quizzes are popular online, too.

You can take fun quizzes to find out things like "What kind of animal would you be?" or "If you were in the movie Star Wars, who would you be?"

You'll also see serious quizzes online too.

While a serious quiz can be helpful to the person taking the quiz and it may even help your site become "sticky" if you offer different quizzes every month or every week, a serious quiz isn't as likely as a fun quiz to "go viral." Of course you can test this for yourself to see what works best in your niche.

The entire fun of these fun quizzes rests with the descriptions you give after the quiz is complete.

> *Example: A "what kind of dog are you?" quiz might have a description like this: "You're like the golden retriever: Gentle with your friends, open to strangers, honest, trustworthy and always willing to play…"*

Here are a few sample quiz ideas for different niches…

- A "What Kind of Animal Are You?" quiz for any sort of animal related sites. Naturally, you should focus on your target market. So if you run a dog site, then it should be a "what kind of dog are you?" quiz.
- A "What Kind of Flower Are You?" quiz for a gardening site.
- A "What Character Are You?" quiz for any sort of movie or book site.
- A "What Season Are You?" quiz for a women's make-up site.

You may even consider creating a quiz based around other marketers in your niche.

> *Example: In marketing circles your quiz might be "Which Marketer Are You?" and would list "famous" online marketers like Jimmy D. Brown, John Reese, Mike Filsaime, and others.*

Would that be buzzworthy?

Absolutely!

People would certainly talk about it on forums and post their quiz results. You may even get the marketers themselves to jump in and join the fun!

> ## Quick Tip: So how do you build a list from quizzes? One of two ways...
>
> First, you can simply bring people to your quiz page and ask them to join your list (offer some sort of freebie for them to do so). After they finish the quiz, you can again give them the opportunity to join your list.
>
> The idea is that since the quiz should go viral, you should be able to draw a large number of people to your site – and convert a certain percentage of them to subscribers.
>
> The second way to build a list using this method is to ask people to subscribe in order to take the quiz. However, doing so risks hindering the viral effect, as not everyone is willing to join a list just to take a quiz.

Day 25:
Using Petitions to Create Viral TRAFFIC and Build Your List

Petitions have the potential to go viral simply because the issues surrounding petitions are often emotionally charged.

People sign them and pass them to their friends to sign them… especially if the issue is very important to them.

Let me give you an example…

Example: In 2007, United States football player Michael Vick was accused of cruelty to animals since he was running a dog fighting ring (he was subsequently convicted). At the time, people were enraged by his actions.

So what do you suppose happened?

That's right, petitions flew around the Internet – ranging from petitions to the NFL to suspend him immediately, to petitions requesting that he get the maximum punishment. And they flew around because people were so passionate about the subject that they signed them and then forwarded them to their friends.

While strong emotional issues seem to work best, you of course you can also make a humorous petition.

Example: Let's say your site includes some sort of site mascot. You might create a petition to write your mascot in as the next president or other leader of your country.

Note:

Most online petitions, of course, aren't actually going to be submitted to any authority. However, they are useful in that they can raise awareness of an issue. And for that reason, people will sign them – if only to feel like they're doing something about an issue where otherwise they are helpless.

The Michael Vick petitions mentioned earlier are good examples. Signing the petitions served as a way for the signers to rechannel their anger and frustrations.

Just as with quizzes, there are <u>two ways</u> you can build a mailing list with petitions.

1. **The first way (and most preferable method) is to work to convert the TRAFFIC into your subscribers.**

2. **The second way is to inform signers that their name is automatically added to a mailing list when they sign the petition. Since some people won't bother to read that "small print," you're likely to get spam complaints if you go this route.**

<u>Tip</u>: As usual, make sure the newsletter people are signing up for is as closely related to the petition issue as possible. In the above Michael Vick example, a good newsletter would be something that keeps people informed of the Vick case as well as dog fighting and other animal abuse.

Perhaps you're racking your brain trying to think of what sort of petitions people in your niche might be passionately interested in signing.

Here are a <u>few tips</u> to uncover those issues…

*   **FOLLOW the news to find out new developments in your niche.**

    Once you've hit on hot topics that could easily become emotional hot buttons for your niche, go to the next step…

*   **FREQUENT your niche forums to keep abreast of what everyone is talking about.**

    Are people talking about the news items you discovered? If not, what ARE they talking about?

    Basically, you should be looking for extremely busy topics on forums. These are the ones that get a lot of views and replies very quickly. If fights tend to break out within these topics, even better – it means people are emotional about the topic and are taking sides.

> **Example: A few years ago the popular weight loss and bodybuilding forums were in an uproar because a popular weight loss drug was about to be banned in the U.S. People were hoarding and stocking up like crazy.**
> **But they were also venting their frustrations on forums. And – you guessed it – they were creating petitions in an attempt to raise awareness of the issue and halt the ban. The ban went through – but many, many people in the niche signed those online petitions.**

- **FIND OUT what the popular bloggers are blogging about.**

  As soon as you see something interesting on the news or hear about it elsewhere, be sure to quickly visit your niche blogs to see if the topic is being blogged about. If comments are enabled, again look for topics that have lots of comments and heated discussions within the comment threads.

- **FEED the topic to your own subscribers and visitors.**

  Send the news to your list, post it on forums, and blog about it. Is it causing quite a "stir" in your niche? If so, you've hit on an emotionally charged topic.

Now that you have some topic ideas you can start making petitions. You can do so free online. Simply search in your favorite search engine for "create an online petition" and you'll unearth dozens of free options.

One important tip: Be sure to remind people to tell their friends about the petition… and give them a compelling reason WHY they should tell their friends. That sort of specific call to action usually increases the viral effect.

Day 26:

How to Create Ebooks and Reports That Go Viral

We've already talked about how to create content that "goes viral."

Just to recap, your content needs to have at least one of these qualities:

- Highly useful
- Entertaining
- Controversial

It can be all three – and indeed –

Any content that artfully and successfully includes <u>all three of those elements</u> increases thechances of the ebook or report going viral.

Example: You can push the envelope and talk about a controversial tactic in your niche. Perhaps the tactic might even offend some people. But that's the sort of content that's both useful and controversial – and when people start becoming offended or push back against your report, then your report becomes entertaining as well.

Indeed, when you first sit down to create your ebook or report, you should think about what sort of conversations you'd like to take place across blogs and forums in your niche.

- What sort of heated discussions might ensue?
- What will people be talking about in general after reading your ebook?

In other words, **start with the end goal in mind**. Since your goal is to get your report or ebook talked about, you should write it around issues and using language that WILL get people talking.

Launching the Report

Earlier we talked about how to launch your viral product with a bang – namely, you need to get it in front of as many prospects as possible. As you've already discovered, one way to do that is to ask affiliates and joint venture partners to help you.

Since a joint venture partner doesn't necessarily require a commission for any sort of deal you set up, you can probably easily imagine setting up joint ventures.

Example: Perhaps you'll do mutual newsletter endorsements – they tell their readers about your report now, and you'll mention a product of theirs later.

But here's a question:

- How do you convince affiliates to pass around a free ebook?

And since your goal isn't even to sell anything up front (rather, it's to get newsletter subscribers), you don't even have a backend commission to offer.

There are two common solutions…

1. __CREATE__ *a rebrandable report that includes links to other products.*

Here's the idea… Just because you're not selling anything in your report directly doesn't mean you can't include a recommendation or two for other people's products.

If you make your report rebrandable, that means that anyone can take the report and change the product links to their affiliate links. So if someone buys something from the report, the affiliate gets the commission. Meanwhile, your report also works to drive new subscribers to your site.

> **Quick Tip: One way to encourage report readers to opt-in to your newsletter is to create a Part 2 of your shocking report. Part 2, of course, is only available to subscribers!**

It's a win-win situation. Your affiliates get backend income from those other products and you get new subscribers. The viral effect tends to take off – especially when readers know that they, too, can rebrand the ebook and make money passing it out to their friends!

* * * __PRE-WRITTEN BRANDED REPORTS__ * * *

If I can get the programmers to work their magic, my long anticipated CBBrander will be available! There are two parts to CBBrander. I will write "pre-written" sales promos for different niches and you can brand them with your affiliate link from Clickbank. That way – you don't have to write and you click a button – and voila' you get a professionally written report branded with your affiliate link! It's brilliant.. so let's hope the programmers can work their magic! Visit www.CBBrander.com

2. <u>CREATE</u> a "pay per lead" commission for your affiliates.

Another common way to get affiliates involved in your viral marketing launch is to offer a commission for every person who opts-in to your newsletter. In this case, the report is ONLY available to subscribers.

Here's how it works…

Affiliates use their special tracking link to tell their newsletter readers about your shocking report. For every person who opts into your list, affiliates receive a small commission – anywhere from about a dime per lead up to a dollar or so.

How much you offer depends on your niche AND it depends on what you have lined up on the backend. You need to offer enough per lead so that affiliates are willing to tell their list. And yet you also need to make sure you can recoup these commissions with your backend offer.

As such, you should test your backend marketing system first before using this method. Otherwise, you could be out hundreds of thousands of dollars with no way to recoup it.

So which model is right for you?

If you're new to marketing or new to your particular niche, you should choose the first model. That way you don't risk your finances on a virtually untested backend system.

Day 27:
How to Create Videos that Go Viral

Back on Day 20 we began our discussion of how to create videos that are buzzworthy and how to launch them to create a splash in your market.

What you learned on Day 20 is enough for you to create hugely popular and successful videos. But here are a few more tips to really catapult your viral video…

- *POST your videos everywhere you can.*

  This includes posting your video on social networking sites (like on Facebook and Twitter) and bookmark the video on social bookmarking sites like Digg, Del.icio.us.

- *PREPARE short videos.*

  If you have a lot to say and do in your video, then break it up into a series of shorter videos. Ideally, very short videos are best – about a minute long.

  Think of it this way…

  How often does someone tell you, "Hey, you just have to watch this 10 minute video?"

  In the "get every thing fast" Internet Age, that's like handing someone a copy of the huge book "*War and Peace.*"

  Now compare that to how often someone sends you a link to a 30 second or one minute video.

  You get those more, right? That's because everyone has time to set aside 30 seconds or so to watch a video. Short videos increase viewership – and encourage viewers to pass them along to their friends.

- ### *PICK your video title and thumbnail pictures carefully!*

You want your video title to get attention – but it should also include your keywords. On YouTube you can change your titles and keywords, so don't be afraid to go back and "tweak" them to increase views.

Some people watch videos depending on what the thumbnail of the video looks like. You can choose a beginning frame, middle frame or the last frame of your video to display on YouTube. Pick the most visually interesting. And indeed, when you create your video you should ensure your thumbnail frame is eye-catching!

- ### *PROVIDE plenty of room for heated discussion.*

When you create your video, create it with the goal of stirring controversy. And then when controversy and heated discussion erupts on YouTube, forums or elsewhere… encourage it!

> **Quick Tip: ASK your subscribers, blog readers, forum friends and others to comment on your YouTube video. If you don't ask, few actually will do so on their own. But once you get comments going (especially a heated discussion), more people are willing to jump in and join the discussion.**

- ### *PUSH your video like crazy!*

If you can hit the "most viewed" page on YouTube, then even more people will see it… and it will truly go viral. That means you need to push (market) your video with the gusto of a bull running down the streets of Pamplona!

- ### *PERFECT the process by hiring professionals!*

   Yes – you can actually outsource the distribution of a "viral" video. That's because most videos don't go viral on their own. No matter how good the video is, it absolutely needs to be marketed heavily to have the best chance for the viral effects to kick in.

   If you're unwilling or unable to do it yourself, there are firms that specialize in blanketing your video link on websites across the 'net. You can search for them online – or go to a freelancing site like elance.com. But be sure to do your due diligence to make sure you truly are dealing with professionals.

While videos are the "in" thing right now, they're NOT the only creation that can go viral…

Day 28:

How to Create Tools and Other Content that Goes Viral

When most people think of viral products, they think of videos, email forwards and reports (ebooks).

However, as mentioned earlier in this report, useful tools can also "go viral." We mentioned the Hotmail example earlier. But here's another example that might spark a few ideas…

Example: Adobe used viral marketing to launch their PDF products. The way they did it is by handing out their PDF Reader for free. Indeed, your last several computers likely had the Adobe Reader already pre-installed. And if your computer doesn't have the reader pre-installed, it's ready available as a free download online.

Now, here's the reason the Adobe Reader went viral…

The next thing Adobe did was encourage the United States government to use their cross platform PDF-creating software. Because it was a wonderful solution to offering documents that could be read on any computer, the government readily used the software. And since the reader was free, there were no worries about people being unable to read the documents.

And that's when the viral effect kicked in…

In order for people to read any government documents, they needed to download the reader. Soon lots of people had the reader on their computers, so other organizations (such as private businesses) started using PDF files. The more organizations that used it, the more people downloaded the reader… and the cycle continued!

The way PayPal got its start is another example of viral marketing.

Sure, they offered free money to anyone who referred new members. But the real viral effect took place on eBay…

First, PayPal marketed their services like crazy as a solution for quick and easy money transfers after an auction. It was brilliant – no waiting days for a check in the mail to arrive, and no paying huge Western Union fees. As such, auction sellers jumped on it immediately.

But here's the catch…

In order to send money to a seller, the buyer needed to open a PayPal account. In other words, both people who used the service needed to open accounts. Genius.

Same thing then happened with PayPal as happened with the Acrobat/ Adobe reader. The more sellers used PayPal, the more buyers needed to sign up. And soon their business exploded.

Does that give you any ideas?

Specifically: **What sort of tool, product or service can you create that requires people to "sign up" to use the tool?**

Also, think about what sorts of other products you can create that carry your marketing message, such as blog themes, blog plug-ins, online calculators, software, and more.

Be creative with your marketing – it's well worth the effort.

CHAPTER 6

The N in G.R.O.W.I.N.G.

NETWORK on Social Marketing Sites

Most of what we talked about so far involves "tried and true" tactics for building your list. This section also involves proven tactics, with one exception... these tactics and strategies for growing your list are likely to become MORE powerful in the future.

That's because this section talks about networking on social marketing sites and other "Web 2.0" sites.

- Day 29: Using social networking sites to build your list.
- Day 30: Driving TRAFFIC using social bookmarking sites.
- Day 31: Building a list using free classified ads.

These sites – and the strategies associated with them – have been around for several years already. However, many experts see the Internet as evolving more and more towards Web 2.0 sites.

As such, any groundwork you lay today on social networking-style sites should continue paying dividends well into the future.

Here's how to do it...

Day 29:
Using Social Networking Sites to Build Your List

There are several general social networking sites you can use to network with potential customers, put together a list of "friends," post your videos, get backlinks, post a blog and more.

Some of the more well-known sites include:

- Facebook.com
- LinkedIn.com
- Twitter.com
- Bebo.com (particularly popular in the UK)
- Friendster.com
- Hi5.com (popular in Germany, India and other places)

Other general Web 2.0 sites that allow you to do some networking include YouTube, Yahoo! Answers, Squidoo, HubPages and similar social media sites.

The good thing about most of these sites is that even though they attract a wide variety of people, you can seek out niches by searching for keywords and seeking out people who are interested in certain types of activities.

You can also seek out (or create) groups, blogs and forums centered around specific interests like weight loss, extreme sports, music, etc.

But don't stop with the well-known general social networking sites. There are plenty of niche sites that may not get as much TRAFFIC or have as many members, but the members are highly targeted.

Example: Dogster.com and Catster.com cater to dog and cat lovers, respectively. You can also find social networking sites in a wide variety of niches and markets including sites for moms (CafeMom), wine lovers (BottleTalk), fashion (GirlSense), hip-hop music (CrackSpace), travel (TravBuddy)… and almost any niche you can think of.

Note:

Before you start using any of these sites to promote your newsletter, be sure to read the site's terms of service. Some of these sites (such as Myspace) have terms that frown on and in some cases prohibit certain commercial activities, which is why Myspace is dying and will soon be a "Geocities-like" ghost town.

Even though these sites differ in the small details, the overall idea is the same.

Namely, you join the site and network with others to build a list of "friends" who share your interests. As a marketer, you of course will be working to build a network of "friends" in your particular niche.

The longer you spend on a particular site, the bigger you can grow your friends list – and the more opportunities you'll have to promote your site.

Many of these social networking sites allow you to post a "bulletin" to your friends, which is basically an internal mass email on the site. And of course many of these sites allow you to keep a blog on the site, which is yet another way for you to keep in touch with your market, promote your newsletter, etc.

As mentioned before, you need to tread carefully and stay within the terms of service when you start promoting yourself.

However, **your goal is to <u>move people</u> from your list of friends <u>to your newsletter list</u>**.

To do so, you need to **give them a compelling reason (and a freebie) to convince them to join**.

And, ideally, you should do this at every opportunity – do it on your main page, on your blog entries, and in your bulletins. Since many sites won't allow you to outright market, you'll need to treat these sites as you would your participation on a niche forum. That is, you provide good content… and drop a signature link at the end of your bulletins, personal emails, forum posts, blog posts and any other activity you engage in on the social networking site.

> **Quick Tip: The conventional wisdom (as described in this section) is to network on these sites to drive TRAFFIC and subscribers to your site. But here's a thought…**
> **Why not create your OWN social networking niche site?**

You don't want to go up against Facebook. However, you certainly can compete in – and dominate – almost any small niche market. And in doing so, you'll naturally build a list of thousands or even hundreds of thousands of prospects!

Day 30:
Driving TRAFFIC Using Social Bookmarking Sites

Another way to drive potential subscribers to your site is by social bookmarking pages of your site.

DEFINED: "Social Bookmarking"

"Social bookmarking" is a way for people to organize and share their bookmarks – also known as their favorite sites online. When you bookmark a site, you can add "tags" (keywords") to the bookmark so that others know what the site is about… and so that people searching for those keywords will find your bookmark.

The more people who bookmark a particular site, the higher it rises up the rankings on the social bookmarking site.

As such, bookmarking bland web pages isn't going to help you out.

What you need to do is bookmark your viral content – your crazy videos and your shocking reports and articles.

Indeed, you should make it easy for people to bookmark your viral content.

Most of the popular bookmarking sites allow you to place their buttons on your site, which means people who have accounts at these popular services can bookmark it with one click.

Like anything in marketing, it's always a good idea to create a call to action.

Specifically, **tell visitors that you WANT them to bookmark your site**. Doing so will help your viral content "go viral."

<u>Quick Tip</u>: Sometimes you need to jumpstart your bookmarking. When you email your list about your content, ask them specifically to bookmark. Likewise, if you blog about it or post on forums about your content, ask people to bookmark it.

You may even consider forming "bookmark rings" where you bookmark your friends' sites and they bookmark yours. But read the sites' terms of service before attempting to use bookmarking rings.

Here are some of the more well-known and popular bookmarking services:

- <u>Del.icio.us</u>
- <u>De.lirio.us</u>
- <u>Digg.com</u>
- <u>Yahoo! Buzz</u>
- <u>StumbleUpon.com</u>
- <u>Reddit.com</u>
- <u>BlinkList.com</u>
- <u>Spurl.net</u>

Day 31:
Building a List Using Free Classified Ads

Today is the day you visit and start using one of the biggest, busiest sites on the Internet:

Craigslist.org (which gets a whopping 10 BILLION page views per month).

There are <u>two ways</u> you can use Craigslist to drive new subscribers to your site:

1. Start posting (free) classified ads on the site.

Craigslist.org is incorporated as a for-profit site (despite it's .org name). However, many users of the site are very anti-commercial. They prefer to see one person selling one product to another person… and they report any posts that look more commercialized than that.

> *Example: If you post an ad to sell your car, that's great. If a dealer posts an ad to sell a car, some of the long-time Craigslist users will cry spam and "flag" the ad for abuse.*

Does that mean commercial posts will get removed?

Not necessarily. But because some people are a little too eager to click the "flag this ad" button, you might get reported (and your ad might possibly be removed) if it looks to commercial.

To avoid this, be sensible.

That means you should only post a few ads in a couple regions each day. Before posting anything, find the most appropriate category, look at what else is being posted (especially those ads that are at least 24-48 hours old), and follow suit.

In other words, model your ads after the types of ads that seem to be working on the site.

2. Network with other Craigslist users by joining the discussion forums.

Craigslist has a huge network of discussion forums across topics ranging from adoption to yoga... and everything in between – including adult-oriented forums.

Treat the Craigslist forums as you would any other niche forum or social network site. Specifically, don't spam the forums with your offers. Instead, post thoughtfully to build your good reputation and establish yourself as an expert in the niche. After you've spent some time doing that, you can begin to use your signature link.

For more tips on how to use the Craigslist forums, refer back to Day 19 where we talked about promoting your newsletter via forums.

The "G" in G.R.O.W.I.N.G.

GET Started!

Do you ever read before you go to sleep at night?

If you're nearing the end of a good book, chances are you probably finished the book rather than going to bed at your usual time.

But then once you finished it, what did you do?

You probably said, "*Wow, that was an awesome book!*" Then you turned the light off, rolled over, and fell promptly to sleep. By the time you woke up in the morning you probably forgot all about the book.

That's fine for a bedtime story, but that's the *LAST* thing I want you to do now that you've come to the end of this ebook!

You're probably excited about everything you've read, right?

Great! Because…

**NOW is the very best time to harness that
excitement and turn it into measurable results.**

Indeed, now I want you to GET STARTED applying and using all the tips, tactics, strategies and secrets you've discovered throughout these pages.

You can go in the order we discussed the strategies in this ebook… or you can start with your favorite and jump around.

Let's recap everything you've learned with the **G.R.O.W.I.N.G.** formula:

G – GIVE prospects a reason to join your list.

R – REAP the benefits of JV and affiliate marketing.

O – OPTIMIZE your site for the search engines.

W – WRITE articles.

I – INVITE others to spread your marketing message.

N – NETWORK on social marketing sites.

G – GET started! …This is your NEXT step!

Just imagine…

You can employ just one of the strategies discussed in this ebook, and –

By tomorrow you could already have NEW subscribers rushing to join your list!

Or you can put this ebook aside and say you'll work on it later.

Tomorrow rolls around, and your list numbers haven't moved at all.

And every day is the same… this ebook gathers virtual dust and your list won't grow.

The choice is yours.

But since you've come this far, I think we both know what you're going to do now…

GET STARTED!

Freedom

On your journey towards happiness and financial freedom, you will experience mental, physical, and emotional roller coaster ups and downs. You will grow as you overcome these challenges and obstacles. You will celebrate the highs of reaching new achievements.

Being an entrepreneur means different things to different people. For me, it means freedom. Freedom to live your life as you WANT to live it NOT the way society, government, or other people tell YOU to live it.

You may choose this new found freedom to travel more (or even live in the Alps in Europe!) or you may choose to go back to college or pick up a new hobby or skill like playing a musical instrument.

It's like one of my favorite movies, "Groundhog Day!" If the day repeated itself everyday, and you got the chance to relive it everyday, what would you do? Have you ever thought about writing a book? Where would you like to live? Would you help others?

As you can see the story is still unwritten for me and you. As you begin to implement a few of the days in Traffic Blast! Then new opportunities and doors will open for you. Make yourself available for life-changing opportunities (and more importantly, watch out for dead-end activities and negative talk). Stay cool my friends!

Onwards and Upwards,

Kit Elliott

Hey!

I would like to hear your thoughts and discussions. Visit me at KitElliott.com and leave a comment – introduce yourself. *Let me know how I can help you!*

Join My Affiliate Program at <u>www.SuperAffiliate.com</u>

Discuss Different Online Opportunities and Strategies at <u>www.KitElliott.com</u>

Follow My Tweets at <u>www.Twitter.com/KitElliott</u>

Facebook Me at <u>www.Facebook.com/1SuperAffiliate</u>

Residual Rush at <u>www.ResidualRush.com</u>

Online Resources and Tools Mentioned in TRAFFIC Blast!

Autoresponder Service for Smart Marketers:

Smart Marketers are switching to WealthWorld Touch for all of their autoresponder needs. With reliable email deliverability and easy to use web forms, I use it for all my email autoresponder and broadcast service. **Visit WealthWorldTouch.com to take the $1 trial!**

Join My Affiliate Program

If you are an affiliate or would like to earn additional revenue, then, please fill feel free to join my affiliate program at **SuperAffiliate.com**. We have retired all Web 2.0 properties and moving into a new line of products and services that are converting at a much higher rate!

Mini Website Builder

If you are not a website guru or a techie kind of person, I recommend MiniSitePro which lets you build mini websites in their backoffice and publish them out to make your website look like a professional Web 2.0 style. Save thousands on programming fees and design fees! You can signup for MiniSitePro at www.MiniSitePro.com

Professional Blog Themes (that I use!)

For your blog, you should use a professional theme from WooThemes. I have switched to WooThemes for all of my websites after spending thousands on customization and design. WooThemes comes equipped with a built-in customization dash board that saves you a lot of time and money on programming and design. Take a look at KitElliott.com.

If you click on the "WooThemes" logo in the lower right corner of KitElliott.com – you will be taken to a list of all of the professional themes that I use. I get credit for any referrals from this link!

Pre-Written, Rebrandable Reports (with YOUR Affiliate Links!)

If I can get the programmers to work their magic, my long anticipated CBBrander will be available! There are two parts to CBBrander. I will write "pre-written" sales promos for different niches and you can brand them with your affiliate link from Clickbank. That way – you don't have to write and you click a button – and voila' you get a professionally written report branded with your affiliate link! It's brilliant.. so let's hope the programmers can work their magic! Visit www.CBBrander.com

www.ingramcontent.com/pod-product-compliance
Lightning Source LLC
Chambersburg PA
CBHW071454200326
41519CB00019B/5730